Reverse Job Sourcing Guide

Mo Davis

www.themoniquedavis.com

Copyright ©2020 by Mo Davis

All rights reserved. No part of this book may be reproduced or transmitted in any form or by any means, electronic or mechanical, including photocopying, recording, or by any information storage and retrieval system, without permission in writing from the author.

Published by The Monique Davis inc

ISBN: 9798321467329

Acknowledgment

To my Heavenly Father, who placed it on my heart to write.

Dedication

This book is lovingly dedicated to every individual facing the challenges of professional setbacks—be it layoffs, terminations, mental health hurdles, or career crises. My hope is that it serves as a compass, guiding you to navigate these challenges with resilience and determination.

To my family—Zoe, Ray, and Rashad—you are the essence of my heart. Your love and support light up my world. I love you beyond measure.

.

FOREWORD

Hi, I'm Ninh Tran. As the Founding Member of Hiretual and Virtual Fair, I am beyond honored and excited to write the Foreword for such a powerful book, *Reverse Job Sourcing Guide*.

Here's why this book aligns so well with my thoughts and background. In the past, I have keynoted global recruiting industry conferences including HR Technology, SourceCon, ERE Recruiting Intelligence, and many others to educate thousands of recruiting professionals on topics like "Artificial Intelligence - Recruiter's Best Friend", "Humanizing Recruiting Today", and "Authentic Leadership for Scalable Growth" to move the needle forward in our industry. I quit my engineering job at **Google** to disrupt the HR Technology world, humanize recruiting, and simplify job search. As the Chief Operating Officer at HireTeamMate, I led all the business operations that placed hundreds of thousands of people into high six figure jobs at Google, Samsung, Twitter, and Uber before launching Hiretual and Virtualfair. Today I help hundreds of thousands of recruiters find the right candidates for the most challenging jobs and power the recruiting efforts of the world's biggest and fastest growing organizations like Amazon, Nike, Intel, Paypal. In contrast, Virtualfair helps job seekers connect with recruiters, hiring teams, and talent advisors like Monique Davis to land their dream jobs and their dream companies.

I first met Monique Davis when I hosted the webinar

on "Impact of Booming Economy on Diversity and Inclusion," where I invited her to join the Hiretual Council, a board of well-respected experts and innovators in their fields. Monique collaborated with me on educating the talent acquisition community with research papers, webinars, and podcasts. Monique shines bright in front of any audience and thrives on helping companies solve their most pressing issues.

Monique is deeply passionate about helping job seekers win and win big. Our first collaboration was a research paper on "Being Intentional & Impacting Your Career During COVID". Since then, I have had the utmost pleasure and honor to partner with Monique on many educational pieces that change people's lives.

How might my story relate to you? Well, despite my successes, I, too, am very familiar with searching for jobs. I understand the disappointments of rejection, the lack of feedback, the black hole of job applications on job boards, and all the trials of looking for a job when you don't have one. I started as an immigrant attending Santa Ana Community College in Southern California, which is in the heart of one of the most underserved communities in the United States. Throughout my journey, I have learned that abundance in friendships can be found even in the most unexpected places and that if everything were easy, life would not be fun.

You will also learn a couple of lessons in this book from Monique's journey in hopes that it will help you during your job search. This book will teach you the strategies and methods to get an edge in landing that dream job and being intentional not to lose sight of the prize.

Take the time and hard work needed to invest in yourself. As Monique says, "Life is tough enough. Your job search doesn't have to be either!". You have a fantastic resource on your hands right now, written by one of the best people who talks the talk and has achieved a lot of success with what she preaches.

Monique and I both made a commitment when we initially collaborated, which was to change one person's life at a time. I hope that one person is you. I only ask that you pass it forward when you are able.

Thank you, and enjoy your new adventure!

Ninh Tran

Co-Founder

Hiretual and Virtual Fair

Web: https://Hiretual.com & https://VirtualFair.io

Introduction

I'm thrilled you took the time to read this. "Reverse Job Sourcing" is more than a book to me; it is a guide to help you throughout your job search journey.

This guide was not created to be a novel. It's genuinely tactically infused with experience from me or my clients. I know that I may have some readers who say, "Code

I researched my old notes when I was on the job hunt. I remember being super desperate, which drove me to make bad decisions during my job search. I hope this book will help you create a strategy that will not give room for many mistakes.

My dream is for you to pull out this book whenever you find yourself in a position to get ready for an exit from your job. I will be satisfied if just one of my tactics and strategies works to help someone.

Thanks for reading!

Monique Davis

Wait, Is this a Lay Off??

I've always been a "storyteller". It was my way to break the ice or make someone laugh who may have had an awful day. So as I wrote this book, I thought, "What better way to help you understand Reverse Sourcing than through stories I've experienced."

I remember these words as if they were just spoken to me, "Monique, we need to talk. Dial into the conference line at noon your time."

Those words came from a new HR executive that had just started with the company about 7-8 months after I began working there. Let's call this company, TelecomCorp. So TelecomCorp's headquarters was in Northern USA, and I lived in Georgia, which meant that I worked remotely with about 30% travel. As I prepared for the call, I was sitting on my comfy sectional, remembering how excited I was about joining the company eight months prior.

This appointment didn't feel like a comfy couch meeting, so I began to move my laptop to my office space in the dining room for more appropriate sitting arrangements. The funny thing was, I had been almost expecting this conversation after recently having a dream that I was being let go due to budget constraints.

I had 30 minutes before the phone call, so I used that

time to think about how I got into this spot. Before working for TelecomCorp, I worked for a fantastic company. We can call them Telecom SuperStars. I was always a bit of a workaholic. If I had to choose between a movie date or finishing a project, I chose

the project. I believe it was the strategic hunt of Talent Acquisition and Recruiting. I loved sourcing, getting lost down those rabbit holes, and deep-diving into the internet to find hidden candidates and then persuade them to join the company. It felt great.

I remember working at Telecom SuperStars as a Talent Acquisition Manager who made a name for myself by training my junior recruiter team on sourcing & hiring hundreds of OSP & ISP telecom teams for a massive two-year national telecom buildout.

I discovered that good recruiters shine, but great recruiters (and leaders) show others HOW to shine.

Recruiting for me at the time wasn't just sitting in front of a desk. I wanted to know first hand where the front line talent worked, their thought process, where they hung out, and what a realistic job preview looked like for them.

I would go on-site and look for the high performers because I wanted to find the exact persona type to recruit more. At Telecom Superstars, they gave me the liberty to do those things. I loved that job.

But just as I was getting comfortable, Telecom Superstars was acquired by another company. The dynamics within management changed drastically.

Tools, resources, support... all changed. Once my salary took a big hit, I began creating an exit strategy to leave the company I had grown to love.

Before I left, I remember having a transparent conversation with one of my internal hiring managers for Telecom SuperStars and just expressing to him that I wouldn't be there for too long because of all the new changes. He simply smiled and stated, "Change doesn't always feel good, Monique, but all good things come from change" It stuck with me. On my way out, I replaced my management position with 2 Senior Recruiters. I received a commission because I replaced them from the staffing agency that I decided to work for after leaving Telecom Superstars.

Eventually, one of the leaders at Telecom Superstars left and went to TelecomCorp. I applied for a Talent Acquisition Manager role there and was hired, which leads me to where we are in the story now.

The call is happening now. After our cordial intros, the HR executive told me that they are outsourcing the entire Talent Acquisition division to India due to budget constraints. I would be a part of that layoff. It looks like my dream became an unwanted reality.

However, I was professional and extremely helpful after hearing the news. I asked, "Is there anything that I can do to help make this transition smoother?"

The HR executive that had been there a cold 30 days told me that she was shocked that I handled this with so much poise, which was strange because she didn't know me from a can of paint. I'm not quite sure how she expected me to react. But I won't digress.

After hearing some formal instructions on what's next, I got off the phone and cried. I wasn't crying because I

was hurt; I was crying because I didn't know what this meant for me.

Suddenly, my life changed, and I didn't have time to prepare for it. I had two choices: I could wallow in pity and newfound self-doubt or wipe my tears and be strong.

Slowly but surely, I began telling myself affirmations.

"Monique, you are going to get through this." "This is just another hurdle that you can leap over!" "You were made to kick butts at obstacles like these!"

Then, I began to believe the words that I was telling myself. And out of nowhere, the words spoken to me months prior from one of my hiring managers came to me as clear as day. "Change doesn't always feel good, but all good things come from change."

Operation 'position myself for those good things', suddenly was set in motion because my life certainly changed.

I knew I had to start viewing myself as a candidate and asking myself real questions.

- ☐ Was my resume up to date?
- ☐ Do I have my resume on the recruiting job boards?
- ☐ How is my image portrayed on Linkedin?
- ☐ What's the most logical progression in my career?
- ☐ What do I want in my next career?
- ☐ Am I worthy of a better position?

These questions helped me. My goal is for them to help you get started!

Reflection: Write down the questions that you know you should be asking yourself before moving forward in your job search.

_____
_____
_____
_____
_____
_____
_____
_____
_____
_____
_____
_____
_____
_____
_____
_____
_____
_____
_____
_____

Settling in FEAR

I remember my position at Telecom SuperStars, I had the flexibility to work from home and come into the office as well. Everyone had that same option and it just promoted a very healthy working environment. When I left to go to the staffing agency temporarily right after Telecom Superstars, I remember feeling caged in, stifled and not my best self. I performed but I felt a lack of freedom which in turn made me feel miserable. Needless to say, I didn't stay for long, and quickly found employment at TelecomCorp after being at the staffing agency for less than 6 months.

Assessing your wants and needs can lead you down a path of happiness without settling.

Here's what settling does:

False

Evidence

Appearing

Real

The acronym spells out **F E A R**..

When we join a position because we fear that we won't find anything else, we settle. This can lead to a destructive pattern of job hopping until you are no longer afraid to live in your truth and have some form of happiness in your position.

I had a client that I coached on what I call "foundational work". She was in a position that she loved for years, and they let her go after financial

budget constraints. She immediately took the first job offer that came her way, and didn't do much research about the company. My client was just so happy to have an offer. She was at the new company for about 6 months and then leadership changed, after another 3 months with new leadership another leader came in and a whopping 30 days later that same leader quit and there was another leader that replaced him. My client began to see a pattern and it alarmed her, but she felt she should stick around because after all, the company's leadership team didn't have much to do with how she worked, right?

Wrong..

Once they replaced the 3rd VP in less than a year, things began to change. Certain perks and privileges that she began to enjoy were being taken away. She was pushed into a role that made her wear many hats but lacked a real career development plan. Her new leader desired her to be a worker bee and concentrate on tasks not vision.

My client was distraught and felt hopeless. She automatically assumed that because she was past the age of 40, finding new employment would be difficult. So she thought it would be best to stay miserable instead of pursuing other opportunities. She allowed FEAR to dictate her happiness.

Thankfully, she and I met at a networking event and after several coaching sessions, we got her confidence back as well as developed an awesome job search strategy that yielded her an amazing opportunity working for a non profit organization that valued her completely! I share that story because once you get over fear, you won't ever settle in your job search again!

Reflect: What fears have you been holding on to regarding your ability to find your next career?

_____
_____
_____
_____
_____
_____
_____
_____
_____
_____
_____
_____
_____
_____
_____

Sourcing - What is it?

I remember when I had to let go of fear and continue to submit applications after being laid off.

I remember not receiving any hits back on any of my resume submissions and it felt like my resume wasn't even being considered for the roles that I was applying to daily.

But I also remember when my lightbulb came on.

I remembered a strategy called sourcing. I recognized the current climate didn't demand a resume submitting strategy, instead I was missing a job sourcing strategy.

I'll never forget being introduced to sourcing. I was just a basic recruiter without a strong knowledge of sourcing and scouting the Internet.

I thought that the name of the recruiting game was "Post & Pray". Typically, I post on Monster or Careerbuilder and then I pray that someone (a diamond in the rough) will submit their application and my hiring manager will sing me praises on how I found the best candidate.
It worked half of the time, but the "post & pray" method did not last long.
I suppose, in my heart of hearts I knew that there was more that I could be doing as a recruiter. However, with the demanding schedule and the heavy workload, all I could really see was simply getting butts in seats.
Then, I came across two women, one named Misty and the other named Irina.

Misty and I developed a relationship after she became my mentor in all things staffing business. But Irina (whom I never met in person), I read an article she wrote one day that opened my eyes to the amazing world of sourcing. I became obsessed. I only desired to be around all things sourcing and desired to be a Sourcer. Once again I found Irina, I stumbled across Jim Stroud, and found his YouTube channel which led me to find Sourcecon! Sourcecon is a gathering of industry innovators and thought-provoking recruiting leaders for real conversations and real networking opportunities to learn from your peers and experts. I begged my employer to send me to Sourcecon which was a place that enlightened me even more. My first time at Sourcecon, I cried while my colleagues were bored out of their minds. I was having the time of my life! I felt like this was exactly where I belonged. I knew that sourcing would change my life and I'm so grateful that I came across it.

Here's what sourcing is - Process of identifying, searching, and networking with potential hires to place for present or future positions.

Yes, that is the definition of sourcing. However, the act of sourcing on the internet brought the definition of sourcing to another level for me. Following Irina, I learned a Sourcing method called BooLean Search Strings. It made me feel like I had super powers or was some powerful genius that could find any information that may be hidden.

Once I applied these methods to my job search strategy I began to see traction. I was Reverse Job Sourcing, which by my own definition was, "the

Process of identifying, searching, and networking with decision makers and colleagues to become a candidate or gain an interview for a present or future position." Sourcing normally starts on the Internet but it may take you to various places outside of the Internet.

Here are the basics of the Boolean search. You can use operators and modifiers along with key words that speak to the internet.

Common operators include: **AND, OR , NOT**

AND - helps you narrow your search by combining words that you want to show up in the results

For example: *Recruiter AND Sourcer*
More advanced Sourcers understand that a space can substitute typing the word AND but when you're just learning Boolean logic, I've found it more comprehensive when you write it out.

OR - will help you expand the options in your search. When you combine words with OR it will give you one or more of those words in your results. Always capitalize OR in your search string!

For example: *engineer OR technician OR specialist*
This string is telling the internet to give me results that include specialist or engineer or technician in the posts links etc or all three.

Now, depending on how you set up your Boolean search strings, you may need to refine your results. That's where NOT comes in to save the day!

NOT - helps you refine and narrow your search as well as remove certain words that you don't want to show up in results

For example: *Marketing NOT assistant*
This string is telling the internet to give me marketing results but don't add the word assistant in the results

First, let's think about the obvious referral places to source from on the internet and beyond to find jobs.

Boolean search strings also include

modifiers. Modifiers include: " ", *, ( )

Quotation Marks - helps you capture an exact phrase in the exact order it appears. Keep in mind that when you don't add quotations to a phrase the results will come back separate

For example: *Social Media* will give you results for social and media but not next to each other or in the same Sentence but if you added quotations, "*Social Media*" would give you results that only had the two words together.

Asterisk - also known as the wild card - helps you replace a letter or end of a word.

For Example: "*Social Media*" *manag** will give you results for Social Media and managed and manager and management and managing

Parentheses - helps you gather similar words or terms

For example: (*Honda OR Toyota OR Acura*) would be a good grouping of a car search you wouldn't add *red* to that parenthese because it's not the make of a car (*Microsoft OR Amazon OR Google*) are popular companies
You wouldn't add *hiring* into that parenthesis because it isn't similar.

This is great foundation building. We can go deeper into the sourcing of these referral places in the next chapter.

Reflection: What other referral networks do you use? Write them down below.

_____

_____

_____

_____

_____

_____

_____

_____

_____

Hide & Go Seek

Where do you go to search for a job? Yes there are tons of places that you can go, like Monster, Indeed, Career builder, and LinkedIn.

But what about those hidden jobs? They require a little digging, organization and an "out of the box" mindset.

Let's dive in!

Social media platforms were always my first place to go to find work. But I learned that the best place to start is through family and friends. Later on we will learn what to say but let's explore where to go first.

Family and Friends
Yes, we can contact them via text messages, emails, and phone calls, but what happens when names change or business contacts leave companies?

For some, this may hit a nerve called pride. My advice to you, don't let it. Most friends and colleagues don't mind helping you, especially if you did a decent job in their experience working with you. So silence the noise of "nobody wants to help me" and make the list.

I don't know about you, but sometimes my memory isn't the best. What I suggest is, take out your old resume, and create a list of all the colleagues you worked with in the past. It doesn't matter if they were short term projects or not.

When I left Telecom Superstars, I remembered contacts from my first real job in recruiting as a receptionist. I made a list of all the people that were on my team that I supported, and that I interacted with.

I organized my list based on our rapport level. I added the letter A for the best rapport level, the letter B for someone who always seemed to be pleasant when we chatted or connected, and C for those that I didn't know very well but we knew of each other. I reached out to the person that I had a great rapport with first, her name was Dee. I searched for Dee in my email inbox and realized I still had her email address! I found her on LinkedIn and we connected for coffee. In the first meeting, she offered me a job. Turns out she was promoted to Branch Manager over the staffing agency and seeking a Direct Hire placement Recruiter.

There are tons of people that you have connected with in your previous organizations, search them in your email and LinkedIn by company name or first connections.

Make sure you don't eliminate anyone from your list because you never know who they know or what they know.

Social media platforms
The wonderful world of social media means billions of connections that could possibly help you in your job search.

LinkedIn.com is over saturated but that could work in

your favor

Of course LinkedIn has a jobs board but there's nothing hidden about that. Get connected with groups on LinkedIn that focus on your skill set, job title and industry as well.

I have spoken at Georgia Tech's Cyber Security Bootcamp hosted by Trilogy Education a couple of times. One of the students reached out regarding reverse sourcing and how he could reverse source LinkedIn. I told him to turn on his open to career opportunities switch in his privacy settings first and make sure he had a message for the recruiters with his contact info in the details.

The key is to find the Linkedin group that you want to penetrate. For instance, the Information Security Community group has over 400k members. Surely there are people that you know in this group but also decision makers that you should connect with.

site:linkedin.com "information security community" chief

This string is telling the internet that you want to receive results with people I may know on LinkedIn that have the title chief and are in the Information Security Community group.
You can replace the group I found for one that you desire to pursue.
Or you can add a specific location.
Play with the strings below to reverse source the decision makers in this group

site:linkedin.com "people you know" "information security community" "greater atlanta" "currently seeking"

site:linkedin.com "information security community" "greater atlanta" chief

You can reverse source by simply searching for LinkedIn posts instead of LinkedIn jobs. Sometimes decision makers post on their own newsfeed instead of the job board. Search for hashtags as well.

Keep in mind, intentional friend, that all of these strings that I created can also be searched inside of Linkedin.com's search engine. However, I am searching outside of linkedin because it helps me go beyond the limit Linkedin gives me for searching in their engine.

There is one place in linkedin that will allow you to search unlimited and that's your Linkedin inbox. Using Reverse sourcing keywords in your LinkedIn messenger will help you find old messages from companies that may have tried to pursue you in the past but just weren't the right fit at the time. You can search for words like conversation, "schedule a call" "are you open" "currently seeking"..

Twitter.com
Twitter is not only a place to find professionals to network with but you can easily use this to find jobs as well.

If you want to find a recruiter or someone in your same field that has mentioned a recruiter use this:

site:twitter.com tweets "recruiter"

During your job search you will notice the importance of lists! This applies to every search you conduct. Even on twitter! Let's create a list on Twitter of awesome recruiters that may post on their timeline about current openings! I'm a huge fan of twitter lists and they are easy to create on twitter.

If you've never created a list on Twitter, don't sweat it. The best work is work that's already done! Don't reinvent the wheel here. You can google the twitter lists that have already been created and copy. You aren't the first person to start a list on twitter, so why not grab the information and the fruits from their labor? It's ok, this is public knowledge and not against the rules. However, if it's a private Twitter page all you have to do is request to connect.

Here's an example of a Twitter list for

sourcing: *site:twitter.com inurl:lists recruiter*

This string is telling the internet that I want results from twitter that have the word lists in the url and that may include the word recruiter anywhere in the post.

You will be able to see lists of tons of recruiters accumulated on Twitter.

Overall, if you want the best way to search for anything in the world on Twitter, use this super advanced sourcing link:

https://twitter.com/search-advanced

This link is the best shortcut to source thoroughly on Twitter without requiring you to learn all the complex strings.

Facebook
Reverse Sourcing on Facebook can be tricky. You don't want to be intrusive so remember this intel is for you to find them on LinkedIn, in a Facebook group, or add their name and job title to your list of research. Facebook is also restricted to only being able to search for a job title, employer, and location. When you are in the actual Facebook web app, you have to search for one thing at a time. For example, in the search bar, add the Employer's name under people's search. With that one keyword, you can find out who has been an employee or is currently an employee for the company you are sourcing for.

Remember common ground is the key to a response. Being added to Facebook Groups that have employed professionals in your industry will also help. You can search for group members easily.

Here's a link to source via Facebook

Site:facebook.com ("recruiter"|"talent acquisition") AROUND 10 ("Role"|"Job"|"title"|"to present") AND "Atlanta" AROUND 10 ("current city"|"to present")

This string is telling the internet to give me results of maximum number of terms being 10 that can be separated from the search terms in the parentheses of a recruiter or talent acquisition job title in the current city of Atlanta on Facebook

Typical online job board
Indeed.com (one of the best ones)
Of course there are jobs that you can source openly. However there is also a forum connected to the Indeed community where professionals ask questions and help each other with job opportunities.

site:www.indeed.com/community recruiter advice

This string is x raying Indeed's community for Amy Recruiter offering advice

I'm not sure how long Indeed community will be around but, please use the string above for any job board that has a community attached to it.

Niche Based Job boards
Idealist.org (non profit)
Builtinnyc.com/jobs
Higheredjobs.com (education)
Virtualjobs.usnlx.com
Jobs.aqpsearch.com (healthcare)

Hidden jobs aren't always hard to find, but it's just having the knowledge about it. Consider creating a search string to find niche job boards that specialize in your industry

Professional Association job boards
Jobs.shrm.org -SHRM
Careercenter.aaahq.org/jobs -American Accounting Association
Careers-amanet.icims.com/jobs -American Management Association
Tiaonline.org/about/careers -Telecom Industry Association

Find out if there's a professional association that focuses on your industry. Regardless of your affiliation to it, you can usually access their job boards.

Going to webinars and in-person networking events is fine, but what about being able to stand out in the crowd?

Here's a tactic that works:
- Create a list of networking events that are NOT job fairs (maybe the focus of the event is selling a product) just make sure the event is somehow connected to your industry. For example, an ATS Training or live demo to HR managers. If you're a recruiter looking for work this would still be an ideal place to go
- Connect with individuals at the event and make notes of their memorable qualities. If you have a list of who's speaking, research them and connect with them. Ask questions and compliment their presentation.

☐ Follow up the next day! We will discuss later on what to say afterwards.

Online Company Directories

"Best places to work"
Chambers of Commerce
Business focus newspapers/blogs
Book of Lists specific to your location

national (association OR organization) KEYWORD

This string helps you find multiple associations and organizations with the keyword you choose.

Site:org KEYWORD

Site:tiaonline.org (Attendees OR members OR participants OR speakers OR presenters OR agenda OR minutes OR meeting OR directory) ext:xls

Site:fieldengineer.com (Attendees OR members OR participants OR speakers OR presenters OR agenda OR minutes OR meeting OR directory) ext:xls

Colleges/Alumni Group

This category is pretty self explanatory but in case you need any assistance, use this string and replace "cyber security" with a job title or industry that interests you:

National ("cyber security") (attendees OR member OR grad OR student OR alum)

The Power of Words

The term "words are powerful" is literal when it comes down to sourcing.

Researching company information specific to your wants and desires won't be a walk in the park, but let's define what you really want in an organization.

Here's a question I've asked my clients seeking a career change, "On a scale from 1-10, how much did you enjoy your current/previous job?"

They may say, "Well Monique I probably would give

them 6 or 7."

Next, I ask what could make them a 10? Most of my clients enjoyed running off a huge list of what they could change about their previous or even current job.

That question is what I want you to ask yourself. What was missing from your previous position? If there was a magic wand that could change everything, what would the company offer you that it didn't before?

Write out a list of those things somewhere on top of your tracking spreadsheet. Those words will help you keep your eyes on the ball.

Now it's time to dig into the companies that stand out to you. Remember, you aren't settling on this next job so truly finding as much information about the company is vital before applications are sent.

Here are some suggestions for your search:

- During your job search, find a couple of job titles that stand out and sound interesting to you.

- Check out the leadership team within the company you like (you can do this via LinkedIn or Zoominfo)
  - Google the names of the leaders along with words like "work environment" OR the company's name
  - Sometimes, you can find blogs or articles mentioning leadership teams
  - Check out what previous or current employees say they enjoyed about the company. (you can do this via glassdoor)
  - Create Google alerts based on the company and its leadership team names to find out what they are up to and their beliefs.
  - Another tip is to do what we call "Social Listening". Go to facebook, twitter or instagram

and search for posts with the company's name and add phrases like "I hate Company Name" or "Company Name was the worst place to work" or "I LOVE Company Name" "Company Name is the best place to work"

- Last but not least, check out your potential team mates. What does their career track and progression look like? (you can do this on Linkedin) Think about it, if multiple teammates seem to stay in the same position for LONG periods of time, then that company may not promote professional development or implement career succession plans.

I realize telling you to search this and search that can lead to a list of millions of websites. Although I know data is powerful, I'd rather not give you information overload. Instead, let me share with you how to create search strings that will help you in your Reverse Sourcing Efforts.

First let's figure out the correct terms.

Remember Boolean Search Strings - It is an internet search where you combine these powerful keywords with operators (i.e AND, NOT and OR) to find and narrow the results.

Well let's use an example. A search string could use words like "Recruiter" AND "Coordinator". This controls the **search** results to focus only on posts, articles, documents, and urls containing those two keywords.

Let's add some operators to a search string along with some key words about the type of decision maker you are looking to find out about:
"Vice President" (Microsoft OR Google OR Apple) This string is telling the internet that you are searching for a Vice President at Microsoft, Google, or Apple.

From there, you can begin your list of decision makers for research. Keep in mind there are other sites and platforms that can help you identify those names as well.
- Zoom info
- Upload
- LinkedIn Company Pages
- Facebook Group Companies

Reflection: Have you identified company leaders and researched the company's values and missions? What are some words and actions that resonate with you?

_____
_____
_____
_____
_____
_____
_____
_____
_____
_____
_____
_____
_____
_____
_____
_____

I Found You, Now What?

Starting off with a list of 20 companies and their leadership teams would be a great foundation to dig into. Once you've done the research, it's time to reach out and build a rapport.

I don't believe that there is a cookie cutter way to reach out to each person. However, I do believe that there is a method or blueprint that can be followed. Below you will find some blue prints that I'd like

The best place to email someone pertaining to a job would be online forums and LinkedIn and the next best place would be a networking event (virtual or in person).

Let's tackle connecting on LinkedIn first because it can be pretty tricky during this time.

There are millions of users on LinkedIn. You will not be the first to have this bright idea to ask for help in your job search. With so many decision makers and HR professionals getting hit up in their inbox time and time again, you have to connect without immediately asking for job help.

I remember a gentleman that connected with me on LinkedIn on Monday and by Tuesday morning he was reaching out to ask for help in his job search.

I replied to his request and stated that I would look around and let him know if I had any positions that may be a good match for him. I also asked what his ideal job title would be.

He responded quickly and said "Well can't you just introduce me to xyz at Delta?"

I took a step back just to make sure I read what he wrote accurately. After that, I took a look at his LinkedIn profile to see who our mutual friends were and how long I had known him. I reviewed all of this because in my mind I was thinking, with that type of tone, we must know each other or have a friend in common.

However, there was no common ground. No rapport built, and no mutual connections. I stopped in my tracks and thought, "What would make him think that he could reach out and just ask to be referred to that level of leadership without me having at least one conversation with him?".

I responded by sending him a link to my calendar. During our conversation I told him I don't typically send out blind referrals. Anyone that I refer to someone else, I preferred to have a conversation with and have clarity on what they are seeking to do career wise. At the end of the day, my name would be on the line and quite frankly I didn't know him well enough to do that.

Of course, I have a heart for those that are seeking employment, so I gave him some pointers on our call and asked how his "tactics" had been working prior to reaching out to me. He told me that he tried the "introduce me to your leaders", to all of his new connections and so far out of 50 outreaches, I was the only one that scheduled a call with him.

I laughed. I felt a teachable moment coming on, so I asked him, "Are you married?".

He chuckled and I felt him blush through the phone as he answered yes.

"Before your first date, did you ask your wife to marry you?" I inquired.

He said, "Of course not, she was out of my league."

I said, "Ok what do you think would have happened if you did ask her that?"

"I'm sure she would have told me no and probably never given me a chance to date her", he responded.

I simply replied with, "Exactly".

Finding your way into your next career with all of this fierce competition around you is very similar to finding your way into the beautiful woman's heart that you know has something special but you can't just outright ask her to marry you. You have to be different and stand out. Even though your ultimate goal may be to get married.

We had a nice conversation and stayed connected. Although I didn't refer him to the leader from Delta that he was seeking to connect with, I did tell him about a position that I knew about and believed matched his skill set and talent. I connected him to the recruiter over the requisition and the good news is, he got the job!

Now, let's dissect the conversation a bit. Do you see yourself in any part of that conversation? What about the blind email requesting a stranger to connect you with someone in their friends list?

Believe it or not, that spells D-E-S-P-E-R-A-T-E. In the job search, even if you are DESPERATE, you don't want to appear that way.

If you have a choice, and you can help it, start your job search while you have a job.

If not, and you are currently unemployed, try your best not to ask immediately for a job from a stranger.

I always say go to your ex- coworkers, colleagues, friends, and family FIRST not last. Remember, it's all in the messaging AND the connection.

Let's say you are asking for help from a previous co worker, send a short text or email like this:

"Hi ____

How are things going? I've been staying connected with you on LinkedIn and it looks like you are up to some pretty cool things.

Don't know if you are aware, but I am currently on the job hunt for a position in (industry). Ideally, I'm looking to (whatever you really want to do within your new position).

I know you have always been well connected and was hoping to pass my resume along to you in case you hear of anything that sounds like it would be a fit.

Of course, if you need anything from me just ask as well.

We had some great times working at _____. Hope

you are still being the (add a characteristic that describes this person, encourager, comedienne, leader, etc). Chat soon."

The message above is perfect even for a previous manager. No one knows your work ethic better than someone you formerly reported to or that you worked with on various projects together.

You may be thinking, "Monique, I worked alone." Or "I don't have anyone to reach out to and ask for help." In that event I'd say it's time to get socially creative. You have two choices, you can create a post on social media that says you are currently seeking employment or you can have a friend post for you. I've seen success in both but you have to do it right.

For instance, comedic memes always get attention. You could post a funny meme like "Fresh Homemade Cookies (if you interview me)"

Or

Creative, direct and to the point. "Excited about having a fresh new start!" Or "Looking for a new adventure that includes slaying data analytics and winning over stakeholders.."

If you do decide to post on your own, get buy-in from a couple of colleagues or friends who will repost your message on their newsfeed for you too.

The next individual that you may want to reach out to could be someone who is currently working in your ideal job, at your targeted company. Need to find them? Not a problem, let's go ahead and create a sourcing search string. First make sure you X-ray the site that you want to find them on. The most popular site to X-ray is LinkedIn.

When x raying any site (we can use LinkedIn), it starts like this:

site:

Then you want to add the different job titles that they could go by depending on the company. For example:

("Data analyst" OR "data manager" OR "data scientist")

Adding the company name is important because you can start to get a feel of who reports to who by focusing on one company at a time. You can also identify what the specific titles are in that company for the job you're
looking for.

You also want to make sure you're adding the location in the same way that it's used on the specific site you're xraying. For example, if you are x-raying LinkedIn, they use phrases like "Greater Atlanta area" when speaking about the entire Atlanta Metro area. You may want to add that phrase to quotations with your sourcing search string.

The full string may look like this:

site:LinkedIn.com "Great Company" ("Data analyst" OR "data manager" OR "data scientist") ("greater atlanta area" OR "Atlanta, GA")

This sourcing search string says, "Give me the internet results for anyone with a profile on LinkedIn, whether I'm connected to them or not, that works for Google as a Data Analyst, Data Manager, or Data Scientist in the Atlanta GA area."

Did you find what you were looking for? I'm sure you

did!

Remember if you start to get results back that include jobs that's fine but you don't need that right this second. So use the not operator or - symbol along with job or jobs to clean up the results.

You can also always add this to make sure your list is cleansed of all the multiple profile page results clustered in one post:

-job

So to clean up your list, please add the "*NOT*" operators at the end like this:

site:linkedin.com "Microsoft" ("Data analyst" OR "data manager" OR "data scientist") ("greater atlanta area" OR "Atlanta, GA") -job

So the final sourcing search string says, give me the internet results for anyone with a profile on LinkedIn whether I'm connected to them or not, that work for Microsoft as a Data Analyst, Data Manager, or Data Scientist in the Atlanta GA area but not the word job in it.

Ok, we should have the right list of similar professionals that match your reverse source search.

Now let's reach out.

Here's an example email to guide you.

"Hi _____,

I'm _____. I had to stop and connect with you because it seems like we have a couple of things in common, especially as it relates to the _____ industry. *(Throw in anything that you liked about their posts or profile)*

I'm a (job title), and currently exploring new opportunities within a (finance/e-commerce/healthcare etc.) position in (location or remote). If you hear of anything like this please, let me know.

Even if you don't have any opportunities that you know of, thank you for being someone that I felt comfortable approaching!"

The above message helps you because you are specifically asking for help within a certain industry and work environment.

There are also certain platforms that some professionals would say to stay away from, but I have to admit that all's Fair in Job searching.

Remember the groups that I mentioned earlier as referral networks. They can exist on Facebook or LinkedIn.

If you are utilizing Facebook, my suggestion would be to source a separate list of contacts. Make sure you have a spreadsheet that includes Name, Contact, Employer, Location, and Notes (with something unique to help you remember them).

Identify them easily on your friends lists. Keep your list streamlined with people that are aligned with your interests. If they are hip hop rappers and you are looking to become a data scientist, that may not be the best contact to add onto the spreadsheet.

Then highlight the ones that you feel the most comfortable with speaking to.

This can be repeated in Facebook groups that you are in as well. Especially if it's an alumni group or previous workers of your ideal company.

The key to networking is not always about asking for

help in the job search. But it's connecting and learning

about what others do, what their needs are, and figuring out ways to help them.

Yes, this is still a book on how to Reverse Job Source. However, it's vital to establish that you not only have a hand out but you are also desiring to lend a hand.

All of the information we've shared is still apart of the foundation. Let's do a quick check list of all the lists that you learned to source.

- List of Ideal Companies to Work for
- Company Leadership lists with details and notes on whether or not they would be a good fit
- List of Current Professionals on your approved Companies list
- Facebook lists of connections to network with
- Email blueprints scripts

Once you have your company lists together along with your blueprint scripts, it's still not time to reach out yet. Yes, we are still building your foundation.

Take a moment to reflect: Did you take the time to create a list with the sourcing methods shared? What were your results?

_____
_____
_____
_____
_____
_____
_____
_____

Social Positioning

Imagine this. You created the perfect contact list, along with the perfect blueprint script. You reach out to a colleague or decision maker and they say, "Why yes, yes, we are looking for someone exactly like you." They ask for your resume, you send it over.

Except while you're sending over the resume, he/she is scrolling through your social media pages, LinkedIn, Facebook etc to get a "feel" of who you are because after all, they don't know you quite yet. They come across some compromising photos with vulgar, inappropriate & offensive language.

Now if you were working for a startup company filled with others that partied just as hard then they would scroll right by and maybe not think twice. But this company is your next level ideal company, with a hint of conservative culture.

The recruiter or decision maker says thanks but no thanks. You missed your chance.

Now of course the recruiter would never tell you that this was the reason but I've seen it happen countless times.

Your best chance is to keep your personal profiles PRIVATE and clean up your public profile pages.

I remember being up for a position at a very conservative company. At the time, I thought this was my dream job! I had my research about the leadership team, I knew exactly how I was going to impress them during my second interview and had aced my first round. I knew this job was a slam dunk.

As I was picking out my second interview outfit, I remember thinking this was it! I was finally going to be employed with this amazing company. My phone rings and it's the recruiter. She sounded sad and told me that the VP was really interested in having a brand ambassador/face of the organization and that she didn't believe I was a right fit. I cried for at least a week. I couldn't quite let it go because this felt so wrong. So I remembered a colleague that previously worked for this company and begged her to get me some intel. Long story short, she mentioned that I should google myself. I remember saying something like whatever they found is not me I haven't done anything to anyone! She was quiet.

And I replied to the awkward silence and asked "Can you please tell me what I did wrong?"

I began to research myself while on the phone with her. I looked and saw nothing significant about me but my old IMDb page and some acting headshots. I remember frantically looking and telling her I don't see anything except some old acting profiles.

She responded and asked, "Are you still pursuing acting?"

I paused and said "Well, not full time, but I do family friendly projects every blue moon.. it's a hobby.."

She ended our conversation by reiterating that they were seeking a company focused Branding Ambassador oriented Talent Acquisition Manager and that I should just be happy that I was in the running. I was not happy, but I did have an "Aha moment!".

Basically, I didn't research the company well. I didn't look at workplace culture or ask the right questions to

ensure that this was the right company for me. So when my acting past (that I was very proud of), came back as a negative instead of a positive, I knew that it was not the right company for me.

There are a couple of reasons why a future employer researches you before hiring.

1. For a workplace culture fit
2. For your social behavior and professionalism
3. Find out how vested you are in your industry

It may not seem fair but it happens and the best way to overcome it, is to prepare for it.

The first thing I'd advise anyone to do in order to position themselves properly, is making sure you know the environment and company culture that you desire as mentioned previously.

Then google yourself. Make sure you delete the old pics and profiles that came up. If you have a social media page that may be deemed risqué or offensive, consider making your profile private during your job search. In my case, the company was very conservative and not looking for anyone that had hobbies outside of the box.

We have to remember what the hiring manager and company are looking for in a hire. The hiring manager is seeking a professional image, dynamic personality, and background information that matches the resume. As long as you can keep that as your main focus, the rest is easy.

Let's go over each platform with tips and tricks to guide you to success.

LinkedIn

LinkedIn Photo: Make sure you have a professional, clear photo. If you are looking for pose inspiration, take a look at your targeted companies list. Check out profile photos of current employees in that prospective department and use that as a blueprint. (remember blueprint doesn't mean that you shouldn't stand out in your own style)

Also, to make your profile even more searchable, save your photo on your desktop as the title of the job that you are looking for. For instance, when you normally save a photo, it saves as Image9840.jpg but you want to save it as TalentAcquisitions.Monique.jpg instead. This will help push your profile to the top when someone is searching for talent acquisition professionals.

This is what I like to call L.E.O. (LinkedIn Engine Optimization). LinkedIn is like its own google, and just as there are search engine optimization strategies for

Google, there are also the same for LinkedIn.

L.E.O.: Being successful in your job search means that your profile must be viewed every time someone searches for the role that you're seeking. Having your profile ranked high is a result of LEO. We mentioned the LEO trick regarding saving your profile photo.

There are a couple of others that I think would help you in your job search positioning.

Particularly skills and endorsements. Make sure that the most important skills are selected on your profile. LinkedIn data confirms that profiles with at least 5 or more skills selected get contacted up to 33 times more than others who don't have skills listed. Remember that list you started with all the names of the individuals that are working in the department at the company you are pursuing? Use that list of current employees and research their current skills. Those are the skills that it takes to work for that company, you should make sure you have them and then list them on your profile. Organizing your skills helps your profile ranking as well. Yes, you can edit your skills listing. Feature the top 3 skills you have that have the greatest endorsements. Feel free to rotate the skills that are popular and delete the ones that are irrelevant.

LinkedIn Headline: Of course LinkedIn automatically adds your job title as the headline, but you can edit it to your liking! Think of this as your career seeking statement. What are some requirements your future position has? PMP certification? SHRM membership? A+ certificate? Adding important certifications in your headline can attract your ideal company. If you speak directly to what the decision makers are looking for, that's another sure way to grab their attention. For example, if I'm an operations manager seeking a project manager. A headline that says, "*PMP Certified Project Manager w/ extensive experience managing multi million dollar complex projects using Agile methodology for aerospace companies.*"

LinkedIn Url: Change your LinkedIn profile url to your name instead of those numbers that you automatically get. This helps previous colleagues find you better as well.

LinkedIn Summary: Use the summary area to add keywords from the Job Description. Think about technical expertise, specific tools, and software that would help your summary stand out to the hiring person.

There are a few different types of summary statements:

Accomplishment focused summaries should mention all sorts of ways you helped a company grow.

Here are a couple of achievements to mention:

- Increased revenue for the company
- Increased productivity for the company
- Identified solutions for problems
- Created & Implemented procedures or systems
- Promotions and Recognitions awarded
- Volunteering for worthy causes

Here's an example of how an accomplishment oriented summary could go:

"I'm a Senior Talent Acquisition manager that thrives on building centers of excellence for technology companies. In developing and managing all recruiting activities for xyz company, I've implemented recruiting strategies surrounded by behavior & personality intel, social media sourcing, and succession planning that increased candidate flow over 400%.

My accomplishments that I'm proud of include:

- Reducing vendor and contingency fees of $200,000
- Implemented Job Snippet videos for Social Media Platforms and created utm links that brought about an increase in the quality of applicants by 70%.
- Created a training program in-house for sourcers and recruiters to advance internet mining and social media skills, which resulted in saving the company $25,000 in training costs.
- My Software Competencies: Taleo, iCims, Brightmove, Kronos, Bullhorn, Expert Sourcer, Sharepoint, Visio, Team Development, Monster, Career Builder, Dice, Ladders"

- **Straight to Point Summaries** would be perfect for those who may want to go the conservative route. This summary should basically say something like this: "*I possess over 10 years of experience within accounts payable and receivables. I'm currently employed at Awesome company as a Senior AR/AP professional, improving payroll procedures by using ADP, reconciling invoices, and entering 40,000 error free transactions monthly. Competencies include: Paylocity, Workday, Bookkeeping, Payroll, and Benefits*"

- **Personality-focused summaries** should tell the story of who you are, your personality and how you got involved in the industry you're pursuing. Storytelling gives you the connection to the decision maker and helps you stand out amongst the crowd. A good interviewer is also a good story teller, so try to use those same stories during the interview process too. We will touch on that later on in this book. Skill set &

Experience are just partial reasons for being hired, your personality can sometimes shine brighter than even your years of experience.

Here's an example of a personality summary:

"As a teenager, I trained for the Olympics track and field 400 meter race. I had so many challenges and obstacles against me I lost count. I didn't have the funds at times to do it, my coach lived an hour away from my home, and I grew up in a pretty poor neighborhood with people that didn't support my hunger and desire to do more. Taking the bus, train, and sometimes walking to practice in a safe area took hours. I wanted to quit maybe 10,000 times. I was approached by dangerous bullies and discouraged by family members that reminded me constantly of where I came from, and that I wasn't going to make it. I didn't give up. I kept pursuing. I realized that was my super talent, being tenacious. I put that same tenacity in recruiting and building teams as a Talent Acquisition Manager. I don't have dangerous bullies to encounter anymore, but I do have disgruntled team members, hiring managers to coach, and candidate obstacles to face daily. I do it without sweat. I'm highly experienced in training teams on social media recruiting, identifying issues in the talent acquisition process and solving them, as well as creating healthy working environments for my teams. If you're interested in having an e-meet up over coffee, or would like to hear about how I made it to the Olympics but didn't win a medal, reach out to me at jdoe@awesome.com."

Your personality summary should showcase a couple

of different personality traits that a decision maker would look for in the role you are pursuing. In the above example, I'm going after a Talent Acquisition Manager role. A person in that role has to be tenacious, fearless, and committed to succeed. Can you see those traits mentioned there? After mentioning your traits, always add your super talents towards the end and close with a call to action with your contact info. As a hiring decision maker myself, personality summaries are my favorite to read!

Twitter

My first tip on positioning yourself on twitter, would be to delete all previous messages. There are software programs that can do it for you automatically. Having a fresh new start can be just what you need to present yourself well. Once you've cleaned up a bit, it's time to make sure your twitter handler is appealing to the profession you are going after. For example, @Cuteface123 wouldn't be appropriate but "careercoachmonique", "JonRecruits", or "ProjectManagerJane" would work more in your favor.

You can always use your first and last name to keep it simple.

If your Twitter handle is approved, it's time for you to go public because having a private account won't get you noticed by recruiters or decision makers.

Twitter Photo: Should be the same photo used on LinkedIn or at least the same guidelines.

Twitter bio: This is similar to a LinkedIn headline. You get about 160 characters, so you can't waste this space. Reverse sourcing is also about you being found. Keywords help you get found by recruiters and decision makers. In this area, focus on adding words that someone searching for your job title would look for.

Here's a couple of terms that a hiring manager may search for while looking for talent:

- Job title (obviously)
- Company function (HR, Financial, Marketing etc.)
- Certificates/Credentials (PMP, MBA, CAPM, A+, SHRM, PhD etc.)
- Industry (Telecom, Aerospace, eCommerce etc.)
- Geography and Languages (Atlanta, USA, Bilingual etc.)
- Previous Popular Brands Worked For (Delta Air Lines, Microsoft, Amazon etc.)
- College attended (Harvard, Yale, Georgia State etc.)

Use this example to help guide you with your Twitter bio:

"**Talent Acquisition** Manager (**AIRS**) w/ 12 years of experience in **I.T., Telecom**, and **Aerospace** industries. Skilled with building teams, training, and **high volume recruiting**. Previously worked for **Delta Air Lines**."

Twitter Website address: In this space, you want to make sure that the website address goes to your LinkedIn profile or resume website page. This will give the hiring person a fuller view of your background and skill set. If you don't have a resume website created, I highly suggest a free one with About.me or Wix

Some recruiters won't go near Facebook for Recruiting. However, the others that do use it may be the ones that are recruiting for the position you desire. My advice on this varies depending on how recruiters search for you. In my experience, it's all about the privacy settings. Your posts and pictures can be private but your About Me section and location can be made public if you change them in the settings.

This may seem like a lot but it depends on how much privacy you desire and if you are actively seeking to be found. Personally, I'd say try not to have multiple profile pages but if you want to keep your personal Facebook profile private, you can always create a public Facebook page also known as a business page or a fan page. If you use this it's still adhering to the Facebook rules concerning making multiple personal pages. If you aren't sure what the public can see on your personal Facebook page, you can do so by clicking those three dots near "View activity log" on your profile page and select public view. Review the parts that are public and which ones are not.

If you don't want to go through the trouble of creating the public page, then be sure the update posts that you desire to be public have the globe next to it and the ones that are just for friends have the icon with the two people side by side on it!

Here's a couple of definitions for update settings:

- "Only me" has a lock icon which only allows you to see that updated post. It's completely private.
- "Public" has a globe icon which means anyone in the world can see the updated post. No matter if they have a Facebook profile or not.
- "Friends" setting is self explanatory. All the people that you have on your friends list can see the updated post.
- "Specific friends" is an additional setting that allows only certain friends to see the updated post.

As mentioned with the other platforms, just add your LinkedIn profile link to your contact and website details. There's also an about you page where you can add your LinkedIn summary or Twitter bio details.

It's all about repurposing at this point.

If you desire to add the jobs that you've previously had, add those to the life events section on your Facebook profile.

Remember that there are photos that will be visible when someone comes to your profile page. Get ahead of the search by featuring 5 photos of your choice that will appear on your timeline. While you're in job search mode, try to connect those pictures to some activities you've seen in common during your research. For example, if during your research you came across company wide volunteering pics, make sure you add your volunteering efforts on your featured photo list. Think about speaking engagements or pictures that show you confidently or in authority. This helps decision makers form a better image of you.

Bottom line, recruiters may not even message you on Facebook, but they may reach out from a group that you're a part of or click a link in your profile that directs them to your resume site. Decision makers and recruiters are using Facebook for intel and ways to contact you. If you follow the tips above that specify what to do, you will find yourself available for more opportunities.

Instagram

Did you know that over 1 billion people use Instagram daily? This number blows my mind, but as a job seeker it should excite you! This means there is a high chance that your profile will be seen by someone making hiring decisions. Let's optimize your Instagram with a couple of tricks!

Unlike Facebook, Instagram doesn't mind if you create multiple accounts. This can work in your favor. Create one strictly for personal and the other one for professional job searching. Again, make sure your profile is public and that your profile photo is clear and showcasing the best version of you.

Instagram website link: Just as mentioned earlier, you should have a resume site link or LinkedIn link in your IG profile.

Instagram bio: Well, this one is shorter than Twitter. You only have 150 characters to sell yourself. Make it worth it! Use the tips from twitter to help you with your verbiage.

Instagram posts: Focus on the career and industry that you're going after. Post photos of you attending a conference or webinar or working from home with appropriate pictures. Don't forget about IG reels, IGTV, and stories that allow you to post short or long videos. Use the video features to speak about projects that you've worked on etc. Sharing videos from employers that you're targeting can help you find some kudo points as well.

Instagram Hashtags: This isn't just for Instagram, but I'd say every platform should use hashtags. Searchable hashtags start with # and add the topic that's trending after it. Popular hashtags include:

- #Jobsearch
- #Remotework
- #Currentlyseeking
- #Jobhunt

Hashtags can also be specific to your job title. Just add a hashtag on the front of it (#Projectmanager). Keep in mind hashtags do not have spaces. Just all one word hashtags.

This may seem like a lot of work but it's worth it when you start receiving emails and inbox messages requesting to speak with you in more depth about your experience. Career coaches and Social media consultants can help you with this. Here's an affordable freelance platform to get help: https://Talent2go.io

Get excited! You are socially positioned to begin reaching out to your list of people.

Using the above tips to build an appealing bio is important in your job search. Practice your summary/bio for social media below:

_____
_____
_____
_____
_____
_____
_____
_____
_____
_____
_____
_____
_____
_____
_____
_____

Building Intentionally

Any Job Search Guide that tells you that you will get tons of responses from individuals that you are reaching out to is not being completely upfront. Yes, there are generic scripts that you can use to get their attention as discussed in the 'Power of Words' chapter in this book. However, there are also tools that can help you understand the person that you are building a rapport with a little bit better.

Ever wonder about the personality types of the decision makers you reach out to? I train recruiters on a couple of different assessments, DISC, Myers Briggs, Enneagram & BIG FIVE in order to identify the "right fit" for their open requisitions. Implementing these assessments typically help you understand if this person would be a good culture "add" on versus fit. Understanding team dynamics and what makes a team succeed is another topic, but keeping that in mind when it concerns your relationship building, is golden.

Let's start off with understanding DISC, before we go into how it can help within your job search, let's discuss how it works.

DISC is an assessment tool used by people that want to understand themselves better and adapt their behaviors with others better.

Most of the time, companies use this tool in order to better understand successful team structures, workstyle, leadership promotions, and sales tactics.

Here are a couple of areas where your DISC profile can help you and others understand:

- ★ Communication needs - Which helps in how we communicate within teams
- ★ WorkStyle understanding - Behaviors and patterns
- ★ Developing a selling experience

DISC stands for:

Dominance - which means the person places emphasis on accomplishments and results. Typically, these are the types of individuals that see the big picture, direct, accept challenges and get straight to the point,

Influence - which means the person can influence or persuade others - has an open demeanor and thrives on building relationships. Typically, this individual is optimistic, enthusiastic, collaborative, and not a fan of being ignored or rejected.

Steadiness - means this person is cooperative, sincere. and reliable. Typically, this individual doesn't work well with being rushed, calm, and very supportive.

Conscientiousness -means this person focused on quality, accuracy, and expertise. Typically, this individual enjoys working independently, objective reasoning, detail oriented, and afraid of being wrong.

Most personality types have combination letters of the DISC acronym that help you understand your communication style better. For instance, if you're a D (Dominance), you may also be a Dc, Di, or DI which

represents the other personality types that may have traits within you as well!

When you are attempting to connect with individuals from your reverse sourcing list, your mission should be to understand who they are and how they prefer to communicate.

Now, my grandmother always told me that I had a keen sense of discernment. I've used that to help me in meetings, business deals, and general communication. However, intuition alone won't do it. I believe adding analytic tools like Humantic.ai can always help. Humantic is AI mixed with emotional intelligence that helps by giving you predictive analytics of the person you desire to communicate with.

Years ago, I recall being introduced to Humantic.ai and I was sourcing a VP opening and not getting much traction. Finding them wasn't the problem, because I always use a tool called Hiretual. Hiretual will instantly help me find any decision maker across multiple platforms. As a matter of fact, Hiretual was too good! It helped me create a powerful source string with keywords and demographics that I would not have thought of myself. The results were a whopping 100 dynamic & diverse VP candidates that the hiring manager approved to pursue. So again, with a tool like Hiretual, finding the talent was easy, getting them to respond and engage was the challenge.

I normally reach out to Talent with a very natural approach and gain success by getting to know them and their needs. However, this position was a higher level than my normal requisitions.

I decided to pursue a VP candidate that I just knew would be perfect. I researched him and gained insight but I was super hesitant about speaking with him. I wanted to communicate with this gentleman properly.

The truth was, I didn't feel connected to him and on top of that he had an intimidating profile picture. He definitely didn't come across as approachable. I knew I needed a tool that could help me learn more about him before connecting with him. I discovered a tool named Humantics and decided to take a chance. Humantic helps humanize personal interactions. It assesses every candidate 360 degrees. I downloaded the free chrome extension of Humantic.ai and it connected to my LinkedIn so that every profile page would show how to communicate properly with a person's personality.

Humantic gave me personalized advice without me doing much on my own. I clicked his profile and received his disc profile instantly and his Big Five Personality Traits. These profiles also gave me a greater understanding of his workplace behavior. One of the bonuses of the tool was that it had a Do's and Don't list for communicating to him. One of the "Do's" was to compliment him on his achievements and get to the point quickly. So, instead of my normal "get to know you" banter. I told him specifically about an initiative that I read about him spearheading, and how it was an amazing accomplishment. I also mentioned that his accomplishment was the reason behind me reaching out to him. My client desired someone like him to lead their team on a similar initiative.

And guess what? He responded! After contacting 20 people, he was the one that responded. Subsequently, he interviewed for the role, made it to the 2nd round of interviews but didn't get selected for the position. He and I remain connected and he still checks in with me.

My experience showed me that Hiretual & Humantic.ai can be used for reverse job sourcing as well.

Here's a couple of ways:

- **Keywords**: make sure you add the key words that describe both your soft and hard skills to your public social media profiles. (This helps you get found easier from recruiters using Hiretual. And it helps your recruiter get your attention with the right outreach email from the tips given by Humantic.ai)
- Reverse Job Sourcing: Use Hiretual's basic subscription or free chrome extension to help you build sourcing strings to find a long list of hiring managers. Then add Humantic.ai to each hiring manager's LinkedIn profile and get personalized tips on how to communicate in your outreach email asking for a job.

But let's take it one step further. Use both tools on

yourself. Find out are you easily found and what are the keywords of the individuals in your industry that were found quickly. Use Humantic to figure out your DISC personality. Identifying your DISC personality can help you figure out which personality types are good for you to work with as well.

For example, I discovered that I'm an Id... I'm a mixture of Influence and Dominance. Which means that I focus on people and their problems. Typically someone that's a D focuses on tackling problems but not building relationships.

As an Id, I work effectively and compatibly with S & D profile types. Of course naturally my compatibility would be with other influencers but I also work well with S (Steadiness) profiles because we both desire to be in supportive relationships.

It's all about relationship style, but when it comes to projects and working together, the best profile to work with is Steadiness. The S profile type gets along with everyone in a project or work situation. They normally just want to keep the peace and support.

Figure out your DISC profile and use it to help you identify potential connections during your job search. Keep in mind, the information received from Humantic isn't only DISC profile but it's also focuses on Big Five which is an assessment that helps you understand why individuals behave a certain way.

Use the intel that you gain from Humantic to help you in what to say and how to ask for favors from people that you don't even know. You will learn so much about yourself in the process!

Take a moment to reflect, What's your DISC or BIG FIVE personality type? Grab it for free with the Humantic.ai chrome extension and describe what they say about you. Is it true?

_____
_____
_____
_____
_____
_____
_____
_____
_____
_____
_____
_____
_____
_____
_____
_____
_____
_____
_____
_____
_____
_____
_____
_____
_____
_____
_____
_____

Interview: Getting Ready

Reverse sourcing isn't just about getting information. to get the interview. It's also using intel to ace each interview level. I'm not going to focus much on first interview tips and tricks. I'd like to focus on the second and third interviews. This interview counts even more because you have to stand out amongst a crowd of individuals that are also on the shortlist!

Before we tackle the interview, let's go over what you need to prepare for the second interview.

First, you should definitely be proud of yourself because getting a second interview is a big deal! But it's not the time for you to get cocky, it's time for you to GET READY!

I want to focus on the phone call or email that invited you to the second interview. A good recruiter calls you, but if you've been playing phone tag and you received an email instead the below advice still applies.

Second interview invite:

- Make sure you know the ins and outs of the role. (Ask Recruiter questions for a crystal clear understanding of their expectations)
- Find out if there will be a panel interview or multiple interviews. (Ask Recruiter names & titles of the interviewers)
- Sit down and recall the things that are important to you in a company. (Make a list))

Now that you've responded to the invite, it's time to prepare for the interview.

Use the list of interviewers and get your research done by doing a couple of things.

Company research - Create a google alert and find out what's been going on within the company and the business unit you're interviewing with. You can use the Boolean search string to get that info.

(he OR she) "for OR at OR on OR with" "first last name"

site:linkedin.com (he OR she) (near OR with) "First and Last Name" -profiles

site:linkedin.com ("my team" OR "our team") ("job title") "first and last name"

"First and Last Name" ("my team" OR "our team")

These strings describe a search for any articles or posts with the decision makers mentioned especially in a team environment.

Interview questions: Being prepared to answer tough questions is just as important as preparing what to ask.

"How long have you been with the company?"

This question can be asked to every person on the interview panel. It's not just for knowledge but it's also to figure out what's going on with the company's culture. If they all have been with the company for a long period of time that's a great sign. If everyone is brand new, then you may want to dig deeper and ask more questions surrounding why??

"Do you guys have team achievement recognition? When was the last time you celebrated a team achievement?"

This question helps you figure out if the company recognizes the efforts of their employees. If for any reason they can't recall the last time specifically, then the environment may not be warm and rewarding.

"What's the typical lunch outing for the team that I'll be working with?"

This question helps you see how busy the workload is and how friendly the team is as well. For instance, I worked in an environment where we ate lunch from our desks every day because we barely had time to go out for lunch. It was not a balanced environment. Ask this question directly to the person that would be a future colleague.

"How many of the team members have flex schedules?"

This question will help you get to inadvertently ask if they have remote policies for everyone or if there are special privileges only for certain individuals. Ask this question and really discern if the answer is politically correct or sincere. Remember you aren't settling anymore.

"What's your favorite perk or benefit that only employees here receive?"

This really helps you gather the benefits that appeal to you. If they have continued education benefits, special employee discounts, bonus match programs, gym access, or free lunch once a month.

"How does management measure success and over what timeline?

This is my favorite question to ask, it shows you if your manager has realistic job expectations or not. What does he/she believe you should be achieving and in what time frame? If the request is unrealistic, either negotiate or decline and keep searching. You will never be happy if you are constantly unable to reach your role's goals.

"What are the biggest challenges that the person in this role faces or will face? How did the company help him/her learn from it?"

This question helps you understand what you may also face in this role. But the follow up question shows the level of support the company gives to those that do have obstacles and challenges. This will also lead to the intel necessary for your first 90 day proposal. Another question to help you with your 90 day proposal, is asking directly what the most important issues and/or priorities are for this role.

Now you have all the intel you need culture wise and mission. If you are going after a position with all you have, then make sure you show up with solutions that will make you shine amongst the competition.

That's where the 90 day proposal comes in.. Typically, right around the 3rd interview. My research and reverse job sourcing helped me gain 10 interviews, 5 second interviews, 3 third interviews. In my 3rd interview, my proposal solved the issues and the obstacles that the hiring manager/recruiter mentioned with a 30-60-90 day plan.

My proposal tackled those areas of improvement in my first 90 days. It's all about visualization with hiring managers. It's not good enough to tell them you are a good fit, you have to make them see you in their positions!

Here's how I broke my proposal plans down
- Title of the type of Strategy
- What is the strategy designed to close the gap

of
- Description of Strategy
- Possible Tactics/ideas
- Action Items
- Time frame per item

Keep in mind that an action without impact on the organization is simply a task. So think about those tactics and action items as solutions, but be prepared to speak to how those solutions will save, increase, reduce, and impact the company. If you have realistic percentages like those for the time frame per item. For example, increasing the candidate flow by 80% in a 90 day period.

You don't have to be in a management position for this. I remember starting off as a talent acquisition specialist and having a 90 day proposal ready based on my 1st interview with the company, and I presented it on the 2nd Interview. By the time I got to the car, I wasn't asked for a 3rd interview, I was asked to join the team.

If you believe that you aren't receiving enough intel to create a thorough 90 day plan, then it's time to research. Creating a reverse string regarding general or common problems in your potential job title will do the trick.

("Talent Acquisition" OR "Recruiter") Common (problems OR issues OR challenges) company

This reverse string tells the internet to find common problems or issues or challenges with a Talent Acquisition professional or a Recruiter in a company. Go ahead and add your job title in place of Talent Acquisition and Recruiter. Make sure you put in as many titles that fit what you do in that space.

Having your 90 day proposal is half the battle, implementing and completing it is the other half!

I've seen numerous interviewees present an amazing 90 day proposal, but bomb the first 90 days with a termination letter included because they didn't perform what they claimed they could.

Before I entered the world of small business ownership, I used all of the Reverse Sourcing tactics and strategies that I shared with you in this book. I found great jobs with amazing pay and benefits, but I knew that I wanted to be a business owner and consultant and that's where I love to be. Now I use Reverse Sourcing for business development, which may be another book very soon!

The Reverse Job Sourcing Guide is meant to steer you in the right direction with tips and tricks that not only help you find the right fit position but also how to win the position of your dreams! Everything I've advised you I have experienced or implemented myself. I'd love to hear about how this helped you! I'm also happy to offer you a free Interview Guide to continue your self paced job coaching efforts.

Here's your freebie for finishing the book!

https://bit.ly/PERFECTINTERVIEWGUIDE
(make sure you use all caps at the end of the link)
Let's take some time to reflect. What role do you see yourself next? What are some great 90 day proposal ideas that you can implement for your next position?

_____

_____

_____

_____

_____

Beyond the Job Search

Well you did it! You completed the book and if you're reading this, you've likely been on a journey through the intricacies of job sourcing, maybe even flipping the traditional job search on its head. That's fantastic! I want to take a moment to touch on something equally vital—leveraging your networks and aligning your career moves with your purpose.

My experience, particularly with Forbes BLK in Atlanta, has taught me loads about this, and I'm eager to share that with you.

My journey as an Advisor with Forbes BLK Atlanta wasn't just a step; it was a giant leap into a community brimming with opportunities and like-minded professionals. Initially, I won't lie, it felt a bit daunting. How do I navigate this? How can I make a difference here?

But here's the thing—every challenge is really just an opportunity in disguise.
Once I got my bearings, it wasn't just about what I could take, but what I could give. And that, my friends, is where the magic happens.

For instance, there was this one time I met a young entrepreneur at a Forbes BLK mixer. They had brilliant ideas but struggled to find the right mentors. I introduced them to a seasoned entrepreneur I knew from the community, and that connection? It blossomed into a mentorship that propelled the young entrepreneur's business forward.
So, how can you make this work for you? Get involved. Whether it's a networking event, another professional group, or an online community, dive in. Offer your skills, ask questions, and when you can, be the bridge that connects people to opportunities. It's not just about networking; it's about building a community that supports and uplifts each other.
You know, before my foray into Forbes BLK and even before becoming an influencer, I underestimated the power of a personal brand. But here's the reality: your brand is your story, and how you tell it can open doors or keep them closed.
My brand evolved over time, mirroring my journey and the lessons learned along the way. It's not just about

logos or catchy taglines; it's about authenticity and consistency.

For example, sharing my journey into Forbes BLK, the ups, the downs, the victories—it all resonated with people because it was genuine. Your story, your brand, should be an authentic reflection of who you are and what you stand for.

Don't get on Linkedin or any Social Media platform just to be "visible". Visibility isn't just about being seen; it's about being remembered. Contribution to your community or industry can significantly boost this. Writing articles, participating in panels, or even engaging in community discussions—it all counts.

I know first hand that transitioning in your career, especially when it involves a leap of faith, can be daunting. But let me tell you, aligning your career moves with your purpose and faith (whatever that means to you) can be incredibly fulfilling.

For me, faith has been a guiding light, especially in times of uncertainty. It's not about having all the answers but trusting that you're on the right path. For instance, when I first joined Forbes BLK, it was more than a career move; it was a step toward fulfilling a deeper purpose—connecting and uplifting others.

Every career move I've made, especially the daunting ones, has been driven by a clear purpose. It wasn't just about advancement; it was about impact. And here's the thing—when your career moves are purpose-driven, they're more likely to lead to fulfillment and success, on your terms.

Embarking on this journey, from diving into Forbes BLK to sharing my experiences with you, has been incredibly rewarding. It's taught me the power of community, the importance of a resonant personal brand, and the fulfillment that comes from aligning career moves with purpose.

I hope my story and the insights shared can inspire you to leverage your networks, build your brand, and make career choices that resonate with your deepest values and goals. Let's move beyond the job search and build careers that aren't just successful but meaningful and fulfilling.

Resources for Personal Development and Career Transitioning

Get certified! Some companies offer it for free but if you are unemployed or your current employer doesn't offer it, then find a webinar

Here's one for free!

EEOC certification:

https://www.compliancetrainingonline.com/eeoc_certification_training.cfm

These are 100% free online courses or very

Inexpensive.

Tech Bridge:

www.techbridge.org

Job Search Academy by Indeed

https://www.indeed.com/job-search-services/workshops?from=jobseeker_marketing#jobsearch

Free Online College with Accredited Degrees:

*Christian Leadership Institute

http://Christianleadersinstitute.org

*This is the only accredited online college that I can recommend from experience. Attaining certifications is free, but earning a bachelor's degree is a generosity driven model.

Free or Inexpensive Online Courses with certificates:

Become A Recruiter course
https://www.themoniquedavis.com has a become a recruiter course and other certifications

HarvardX - https://www.edx.org/school/harvardx

Yale Online

http://online.yale.edu/about

Alison

https://alison.com/

Open2Study

https://www.open2study.com/

Coursera

https://www.coursera.org/

Udacity

https://www.udacity.com/

Future

https://www.futurelearn.com/

NPTEL

https://onlinecourses.nptel.ac.in/explorer

OpenLearn

http://www.open.edu/openlearn/

Saylor

http://www.saylor.org/

Fresh Talent Source is a minority owned business that specializes in talent optimization and providing training within a vast number of industries. We are also committed to helping unemployed and returning citizens transition into professional thriving careers.

Want career coaching tips? Reach out to us at

monique@ftsources.com

Reference

Boolean Black Belt. (2015). Free sourcing & recruiting tools, guides, resources. Retrieved from

http://booleanblackbelt.com/free-sourcing-recruiting-tools-guides-resources/

Davis, M. (2018). Respect the Code: Laws for Career Strategies & Codeswitching. [Self-published].

Twitter. (n.d.). Advanced search. Retrieved from https://twitter.com/search-advanced

LinkedIn. (n.d.). Retrieved from https://linkedin.com

www.ingramcontent.com/pod-product-compliance
Lightning Source LLC
Chambersburg PA
CBHW070407230526
45471CB00006B/2693